Roman Pines at Berkeley

by

Hugh O' Donnell

Acknowledgements are due to the following: New Irish Writing (The Irish Press); Poetry Ireland Review; The Salmon; Cyphers; The Honest Ulsterman; The Belfast Review; Acumen; Four Quarters, (La Salle Univ., Phila.); Berkeley Poetry Review.

The poem, 'Maol Íosa Ó Brolchain: Poet' appears in 'Where Aileach Guards (A Millenium of Gaelic Civilisation)' by Brian Bonner.

Cover graphic by Michael Moran
Designed and typeset by *nova print*, Galway
Printed by Colour Books, Dublin

© Hugh O' Donnell, 1990. All rights reserved
ISBN: 0 948 339 35 7 hardback £8.50
ISBN: 0 948 339 36 5 softback £4.50

Produced with the financial assistance of
The Arts Council (An Comhairle Ealaíon)

Salmon Publishing
Auburn, Upper Fairhill, Galway

*I don't remember when I was two
but my parents do
for them*

Contents

I

Sounds Surfacing at 5 1
Letter from my Mother 2
Gardening in May......................................3
Another View...4
Our Street..5
Night Duty 6
Maritime 7
Erosion at Spanish Point...........................8
The Damned 9
Profile 10
Love Poem...11
Spider 12
Disciple 13
Kinds of Poem 14
Self 15
Occupant 16
Dying 17
Specialist 18
Roman Pines at Berkeley 19
Bookcase...20
Maol Íosa Ó Brolcháin: Poet.....................21
Snooker Hall, IO a.m. 22
A Poetry Reading 23
Sunset 24

II

Poetry: a Career 29
New Love 30
Promise 31
Life Study 32
Inarticulate 33
Storyteller 34
My Niece Nearly Five 35
At a Loss 36
February Skyline 37
Resolution 38
Dream of Good Friday 39
Summer 40
Mrs. Moody's Blues See Red 41
Orchard 43
Surreal 44
Arrangements 45
Giraffe at Fota 47
Autumn View 48
Airing Blankets in Donegal 49
Mulladuff House 50

I

Sounds Surfacing at 5

Dazzled by the desk-lamp, I name them:
the two-faced tick of the spy
on the bedside locker, a hiss
from the hi-fi caught between stations,

the bleat of a car-horn overtaking,
a gurgle of conversation, a memory –
the shush of early mornings kicking
through wet grass, my heart beating –

until a startled breath breezes
down my nostrils and the wash
of tidal traffic returns, the evening
violence of keys breaking in next door.

Letter from My Mother

Every second day, nearby
neighbours are shutting up
and moving house
to a nameless street;

she grows anxious: she
would like to keep her own
house dry; she knows
the end is sinister

that it moves in
without a warrant
and settles into
the best chair;

she meets with women
who confirm suspicions:
years ago, there was never any
talk of death intruding;

she leans into another day,
preparing herself to find
the door open
and men there.

Gardening in May

The heart-breaking stuff over,
there is now a compatible air
to encourage green; just now,
a man driving a lawnmower
has disappeared behind some trees
assuring us that everything
is under control; it's a show

of force, all this industry,
a clear statement that we are
alive and notice grass coming on
strong, leaves stirring...
but mainly it's the old year
we inhabit where lives linger
neither happy nor supremely sad;

for seasons are like children,
craving our attention,
showing off their poems
and early steps; we indulge
their promise for a time
until the pressure builds
and we rush out to murder daisies.

Another View

(i) Copper Beech

Since I came back,
the copper beech has drawn
me aside, dipping its brush
into lenten leaf;

occupant of many rooms,
how intimate its dealings
with light, shedding its weight
of shadow on the lawn.

(ii) Celie's Tale

'He beat me like he beat the children'

The farmhands' chopping
has left the windbreak
wounded; nobody minds:
in time the wooden flesh
will heal: trees feel no pain;
Celie makes herself wood,
knows that trees fear men.

Our Street

While the bricks were still warm
from the builders' hands,
the women came to honeymoon
as neighbours and lovers,
the men to settle in the nearest bar;

on Sundays, they shut out talk
of sin and physical decay,
then stumbled home to gamble
on children and what the neighbours say.

Although cars still braked
to avoid a runaway ball,
they saw themselves grow older
and slow down, the small grandchildren
rattled at the gate;

then one by one they parted –
the bed was moved downstairs –
and left as unobtrusively
as they had come;

I left early and wasn't around
when the curtains were drawn.

Night Duty

Along the day's dead march in time
resound the echoes of my father's foot
on cobbled stone: tapping
into the wet light of city streets,
flexing the ankles for 3 miles home;

first to arrive on the burgled town,
the streets delaying on corners
disperse, saying,"we saw nothing,
only the dog return to scavenging
as you passed on";

colours emerge as dawn is breaking,
the watchman's fire steals out,
a smarter step clicks up the garden path,
he turns his wrist, his key
unlocks the door.

Maritime

I

The wet-slate stare,
the gutting knife,
the herring woman
always to the point,
her busy fingers idle
on the scales;

beyond the practised hand,
the slit and cut,
her body netted
in wedding white
warms to the work.

II

The salt air combs
the heady dock at night;
what do they dream of,
women in lamplight?
Hands pocketed, the day

slapped down and parted,
laid to one side,
idling on a list,
the sting of dawn
in the marketplace.

Erosion at Spanish Point

Despite the impish spray,
we do not laugh, but pick
our solitary steps across
the unmade beds of rock;
where will we be, we say,
in a hundred years
on a similar day,
as the black-backed gull
hovers for a moment above
the rotting teeth of a fence
then fades out of sight;

in the growing mist I recall
how a child succumbs
to the trick and treat of tide:
"why does the water not spill
all over the place..?"
while we clamber up the hag-
face of cliff schooled to
a constant trickling of land.

The Damned

The artist never painted them
like this: the free-fall of a million
grinning lives that scatter,
ending their days in the mulch

of neglected drains; their tantrum
before the final shake-down,
the losing heart against the pull
the earth exerts, gravity beckoning;

then their crash (in slow-motion),
the trumpeting oblivion of summer
blush and grace, the whisper
of defeat rising with the fallen.

Profile

In the beginning word shot round
that God was back: creation gasped;
He reached out of the dark with something
to say – sounded like nothing;
He settled for order, "in single file
please": they wouldn't hear of it;
He tried every trick in the book
but failed; withdrew.

In His absence a sculptor discovered
what looked like the all-seeing eye
in a fissure of rock – everyone took to
stone; an arms length away, foot –
tapping with patience, God sharpens
an axe, sharpens an axe.

Love Poem

Heavily laden with light,
contested in the air
on frosted mornings,

it shuns thought like skin-
cancer burning at night,
resisting arrest;

returns to words,
climbing a wisp of hair
on the off-chance

that it might lead somewhere,
uncovering a line;
it loves the privacy

of lingering after clay
has overturned everything,
like a worm.

Spider

The spider keeps to the upper reaches
like a hermit; at certain times,
his rule of life requires that
he extend himself and show a little leg;

he can be seen scuttling from one point
to another, intent on business,
or keeping quite still
psycho-analyzing his prey;

accommodation in the corner of the room
is adequate for his purpose –
as he unwraps another humble meal;
he likes to meditate

but can't help thinking
that if he were a billion times bigger
he could really stick in the boot!

Disciple

He tapped into wood for an echo
of voice, a choice of word, a way
with speech, stripping the bark
white for the bare smell;

counting the cost, nails
and the squabbling to decide
whose hand it was, a haunted
Judas applies himself to sounding

the room for a whereabouts,
anxious to recover that craft,
the striking line, finding another
angle on the stable currency of flesh.

Kinds of Poem

Some leave you hanging
in a kind of game

you have poems of incision
on the jugular vein

there are broad-minded ones
where a lunatic is let out for a day

some make statements
that the police file away

there are poems of love
which tell lies to cover up

some strangle their subject
in the city dump

some are just for a laugh
out of boredom or despair

some publish long-term grudges
from the electric chair.

Self

I have brought my things out of Russia:
Paris has shed its light on them.
                                   Chagall, 1910

I can imagine a painter like Chagall
doing a portrait of me, giving me the space
in which to expose myself, flying above
our street in my childhood wear – everything
too tight – and around me in their exact
orbit my room mates, bed, books, dressing
gown, desk, mirror, a chair for my travelling
companion economically making time;
and in a vast gallery being presented
with this work of art, framed, signed
in the authentic hand with silence falling
on the assembled void – "this is your life!"
I pay the artist with a bouncing cheque,
my last flutter from a basement room.

Occupant

What is this room without me?
Unoccupied, it pays no rent:
it owes everything to me;
being the prodigal landlord,
I am prepared to stay and be
the company that keeps it

sane. I would not wish to be
an empty room; I could never cope
 with the big spaces and nobody
to cross barefoot to take a glass
of water from the tap, or keep
the desk busy, dust from settling.

Now I do not want to own an empty
room, but pity for this outline,
I for the moment call mine,
demands that I remain
and shorten the lonely distance
between here and disrepair.

Dying

Dying is essentially doing your own thing!
what you have been always trying to avoid
and always trying to accomplish; you have

read for many parts, memorised a few lines,
out of character for a lifetime until this
turns up; true, you didn't audition it wasn't

advertised, but the part is made for you,
unscripted, unrehearsed – let the critics rave –
living is completely going out of your mind!

Specialist

'Dr. B. Crennan' in capital type
shows me the door. He knows
the species medically, having studied
life and death as cause and effect.

When you're sick, he can reassure you
that you're not the first –
everyone has his pain,
(it's all a matter of the name!)

You can, unwittingly, fail to satisfy
expectations: then you are left alone,
until you're willing to cooperate
and give up pretending to be well.

You see, this is a healing place,
although people have been sent further.

Roman Pines at Berkeley

They plot the landscape against our being
eternal: they swell, all aristocracy,
with roots and background, centuries
of pedigree; to them it does not matter
that we pass, or snuggle in a splash
of sunlight on the lawn, or meditate
on dwindling guarantees; love is not

their joy, but only wind that leaves
their heads swimming as they toss
their well-bred secrets to the sky
and show their style; as I hurry past

the surgeon who attends, I know
they will not fold with cardiac arrest
from flustered lives; when they go
they leave a rush of light, a memory
of reproach, a folk-tale
of lined faces seasoned in bark.

Bookcase

Why should I find it strange
to hear them breathing
from the bookshelf; thoughts

live on: words dipping their
toes in meaning draw back;
they trifle in conversation,

cough up what's painfully said,
harbour grudges in silence,
standing speechless at the end;

serving a sentence on the shelf,
they forgive us our trespasses
as we forgive them!

Maol Íosa Ó Brolcháin: Poet
d. Lismore 1086

They testify to this in cold faces
paving the decades with starlight:
speaking a language of night, voices
in shadow, Deus meus adiuva me;
at all hours, light is on upstairs,
his grace before death in a sick-room,
"I thank you for what is not a pleasure",
stone-blind, turned towards the wall;
nine centuries on, our theme the same,
our closeness to clay – "It is six months
from yesterday that I have been lying
on my sick-bed.." – we reach for his
words that bear the imprint of love,
like verse in a psalter lost in prayer.

Snooker Hall, 10 a.m.

He is skirting the edge
where the smoky dark
swallows and withdraws;

he angles on a red,
tracking on black,
echoes footfall and pass;

19 tables go unmanned,
the hanging light of one
reflects the green;

shrouded in his own space,
he plays alone.

A Poetry Reading

They leave together, one like a mother,
as the last phrase is tipped
in public; her white head
offers dignity a place;

modestly, she weighs the love-
struck echoes in flight,
will they ring for her afterhours
when she cannot sleep?

slipping off before the party-
talk, just like a lover,
she knows it isn't true, only
death is truly passionate;

she lights a vigil to his
anniversary – the proof of it!
then lets the red wine find its way,
like words on a page, trickling.

Sunset

After a lengthy debate with light,
after the ghost-hunting mist has
settled it for fields, across motorways,
after conjecture – how busy the stars,
how idle the spaces between words –
after headlights smash across
the windscreen and shadows give
the slip to what is real,
after dark, be quiet and dim.

II

Poetry: a Career

Dogged by "whatever happens, happens",
it is not too much to direct that
you drop everything and run off
with the first girl's eyes
you remember – if she is still
around – protesting your love
and this time determined
to see it through;

failing that, to stand in
a public place, and with a total
disregard for tact,
tell everyone you meet exactly
what you think of them,
of their blindness, their politics
and their god, (they will question
the state of your soul)

then before the police arrive,
make for a favourite mountain-top
where, armed with no more
than your voice and a skinny will,
lie down in the heather
and surrender yourself to sky;
if you catch your death,
it will have been all worthwhile;

no matter, it is a formative process
and takes time.

New Love

Through the wood
green-fingered paths
criss-cross everywhere;
the horse draws timber
drudgingly to the lake;
the clapping of strong wings
at fixed intervals is the swan;
there is an island;

under snow, the wood is
love imagined,
inviting and withdrawing in turn,
feeling its way eagerly
to the edge of dark water,
finding a boat;

in the clearing
promises are made forever;
time falters with the rush of wings;
exploring paths lead on and on;
there is an island
and a small boat.

Promise

Words scribbled carelessly
on a black and white photo
with love: what was passed
quickly, while the teacher
broke his lesson into chalk;

during the break, someone scrawls
their secret out in chalk-dust
on the desk – 'Brian loves Brenda'
to infinity, but nothing can come
between these first lessons,
the sharp focus of youth;

closeness becomes unbearable:
they will run away
and be together forever –
no more folded, enigmatic notes,
heartbreaking sideways glances;

something snaps and friends regroup;
then feeling flat and embarrassed,
like grown-ups, pretending nothing,
although still recording a dry taste
after something good.

Life Study

Hers is a study of helpless love,
shading him into her cupboard world:
into a bottle, or kettle, or cup,
his face in an object, his lower lip;

fine and soft lines fold him in,
she has him now, just a touch
round the rim, as under the eyes
and nostril and chin

she feels for the shadow
and draws it in;
in less than an hour
he's coming to –

she would frighten him,
if only he knew.

Inarticulate

In Curragh Chase, my throat is burning
with an April flu, while the tea-time sun
warms my back and shoulders; I am standing

half-way down a pathway by a stream,
charmed by bird-song and, where it overflows,
a pan of water frying; I close my eyes

and dip my fingers in, let the chill
of water smack them cold; I want to drown
my ear in melodies that prisoners cannot hear,

for I am cut off by words from what I know
I love; as I walk away with my cool shadow
for company, the lisp of fluent water grows

fainter, until it mingles with the breeze;
this is the language in which to love –
beyond imperative, close to the bone!

Storyteller

The row-boat creaks as the wind
clambers across it: evening
lifting a lakeside breeze;

like fishermen we sit there, held
fast by the measured voice,
the steady eyes;

the pace is never forced; in his hands
our minds assume the features
of the story line,

details, like silver thoughts, sink
glittering through smoky light
to the bottom.

Lost in the magic of his craft,
dripping with suspense,
he takes us alive

down to places we have never been
with shuttered windows, shadows,
buried fears,

his fingers squeezing a last shudder
of breath from a drowning man;
we never dare to ask him

"Is it true?": It has to be; he knows
the deeps behind delighted eyes
as he draws us out gasping.

My Niece Nearly Five

Cramped conditions favour her at four;
she twirls on a sixpence into dance
routines unrehearsed, broadcasts
original compositions through 15 yards
of green hosepipe for silent millions;

highly amused at her lightfoot sense
of fun, she delivers speeches to her
great grandchildren perched on the fence,
berating infants and mothers alike;

if you can be trusted, she will impart
one hundred thousand secrets only
she knows, giving everything away;
in the night sky she is the star beguiling
your exhausted world with fantasy;

the logic of your departure is beyond her,
but having squeezed the life out of you,
she whispers goodbye inside your jacket
where the lining smells of you.

At a Loss

What I love about you is the way you go
on reading your best-selling romantic novel,
as sickness fans out in a thorough-going
search for signs of life; and how your voice
leaps in recognition as you pick up
the accent on a telephone call – sickness
working the late hours in torchlight,
dipping reverently over broken ground;
what I love is your love for days
you'll never spend deliciously in bed,
planning the evenings in detail, ear rings,
colour-schemes, fingernails – sickness
stumbling into dawn, bone-weary, past
your house with the bedroom light still on.

February Skyline

At 6.30 a.m., I go up on the roof
to watch the moon heal, bandaged
in cloud, observing that wound
of night become a scar,

then disappear; as she moves
in a flimsy gauze – all flesh
is sky – the place of healing
shows and hides, leaving me

higher than the sculpture
of crane, its horizontal line;
across the Bay Bridge
the 'Hail Mary's' of passing

cars thread the hem of morning:
aircraft blink, for here
day is dissolving in a water-
colourist's dream of unaccount –

able lights and accidents,
a woman is raising her head.

Resolution

The brimming ash-tray exhales
as I sit inside drained walls
where smoke has christened everything
and remember how we began
with the smear of wet ash hardening
on our forehead.... "in this liturgy

we are full of praise for dead things,
like the coffee stains ebbed
in the cup..." if only we could
repent, prevent the end of all
our action turning sour..but "morning,
dear", she says and lights up.

Dream of Good Friday

He has been seen snooping
around the girls' room
(therefore he must die)
he was wearing dark glasses
spoke a bad word he said
"bust" (he must die)
he dived through a window
and disappeared
into thin air (he must)
children were questioned
about him they couldn't
say (die)
we have him now drawing
him up on the machine
(therefore he)
but he is not dead just
pretending he has a gun
by his chest (must)
there is no corpse here
we heard him say
in a foreign accent
(therefore he must)
the hill is steep he may
roll all the way down
(die)
the boy wants to watch
with tears in his eyes
(he must)
the teachers are sweeping
up the dead leaves (die)

Summer

Remember the clotheslines, sun
dozing on slates, weeds on display,
neighbours raising a ladder;

the fields in shirtsleeves,
holding hands, dreaming elderberries
in a claret; and inside, a piano

playing ragtime, Julie knocking
back the gin, easing herself out
of the bed another slept in.

Mrs. Moody's Blues See Red

Mrs. Moody saw the wind
shake down apples from trees
and suspected boys;
flower pots overturned
and rose petals strewn about
convinced her;
but when a straying piebald
imprinted her turf lawn
with a novel design, she traced
football boots for hoof marks
and declared war.

Assistance arrived as a uniformed squad
and, under her direction,
the culprits were quickly picked up;
one, while seated on a low wall,
dangling his feet, puppet-like
– playing it cool –
another, in the act
of breaking into his own house:
the third, with a ball,
which lay defiantly close to his right foot.

Sentences were imposed she was told
and the ball was now on the other foot –
attached by a metal chain!

Mrs. Moody returned to her seat by the window
and looked out.

The quiet within unnerves the afternoon,
before a movement takes her eye – "They're back!"
but this time, armed with iron ball,
to drag across her fretting lawn.

Orchard

You couldn't really call it an orchard,
old age among unwanted fruit, ivy
tying it in knots, tackling
about the knees;

in August, the apples to survive
another stealing are scabby, pock-
marked, the best ones out of reach:
from a distance, they glow
like royalty;

it was never worth the trouble,
Dermot said, it wasn't
a real orchard anyway.

Surreal

Waiting in a station as a train steals
past without stopping reminds me that

passing Solomon's Lane this morning
its freshly-painted 'No Bicycles'

prohibition stared at me; and yesterday
among the appealing titles

in a Faversham bookshop when I stopped
at 'How to Grow African Violets',

(the ultimate challenge to the small-
time gardener), I noticed the old lady

watching me; trains move stealthily,
carrying people into a distance of gardens

and small stations, past carefree
cyclists for whom time ceases to exist.

Arrangements

(i) Sweetpea

A handful of sweetpea now bloom
in a mug which says coyly – 'You
brought me out of my shell' –
their tousled heads putting
a tidy room to shame; from sloe

to faintest raspberry they blush,
seducing the walled air
with a fruity tang, inviting
a childish question yet again –
"Mammy, but can you eat them?"

(ii) Carnations

All starry-eyed, they come of age,
flaunting their frills, shooting
their hearts into space, while I

denounce peace for hours spent
watching the tight heads probing,
then bursting in a show of force.

(iii) Snowdrops

Dreaming of wind running
fingers through their hair,
they hang their heads, go off
in sleep; the long stems

snipped, they should fall
flat, but pluck up time
that we're not conscious of;
gleaming in a glass,

they point to a reverse –
we turn to soil, having shed
light dimly in a room, having
scented the bottled air.

Giraffe at Fota

This borrowed landscape: giraffe
listening on VHF to cables whispering

as, sculptured in paving-stones,
they lean up from summer grass,

seeing beyond the smug horizon;
they keep aloof, indulge the thought

of God coming down to size –
'the meek shall inherit the earth'

for when they run they almost fly
like moon-men free of gravity;

their mind on sky, the hours
of meditation seem endless until,

sighing for stars, they find themselves
being prodded inside for the night.

Autumn View

There is no better view around,
potted in every eye by trees;
from the best seat fanfare,
celebration, cheers, high-wire
abandon, clowning about, top hats
lording it for shining eyes;

but when the crowds sail home,
what lies behind in sawdust, scrubbing
make-up, cursing make-believe?;
another month and drains will fill
with forgotten blushes, the room be
vacant, distance drawing near.

Airing Blankets in Donegal

Now they are galloping with the wind up
and the sun on their backs; such Cossack
fury, horse and rider impossibly one;
snorting and kicking, hanging on for dear
life, a flogging will release the itch
of dampness from their veins; ears pricked
among the stony hills, their bright colours
excite with thoughts of giant bats coming
in squadrons; will they ever settle down
to lying comfortless on a bed after the chase
and the effort to edge even half a head ahead;
now with their tails up, I haven't the heart
to take them in, although I fear they will
carry grudges with them to the grave.

Mulladuff House

These were the rooms – a front one
with an air of 'adults speak in here',
the piano with its missing ivories,
the stuffed pheasant, out of place
among photographs and souvenirs;

across the hall, the one that no-one
used, with boxes full of shooting
magazines, an old typewriter,
fallen plaster, neglected walls;
a third opened on a picture of cattle

standing in the shallows drinking;
the dog slept in there – its scarred
panelling looked like a cage –
he never went without a struggle;
in the morning, the bathroom assumed

control, grandfather stooped to enter:
you didn't dare disturb his shaving
hand; in the mirror now, I search for him,
finding summer turning keys in my mind;
year after year, I open and enter.